I'M ALREADY PROFESSIONALLY DEVELOPED

STRAIGHT FROM THE TEACHER'S DESK

EDDIE B.

I'M ALREADY PROFESSIONALLY DEVELOPED
STRAIGHT FROM THE TEACHER'S DESK

iUniverse books may be ordered through booksellers or by contacting:

iUniverse
1663 Liberty Drive
Bloomington, IN 47403
www.iuniverse.com
1-800-Authors (1-800-288-4677)

ISBN: 978-1-5320-6792-1 (sc)
ISBN: 978-1-5320-6791-4 (hc)
ISBN: 978-1-5320-6793-8 (e)

Library of Congress Control Number: 2019901455

Print information available on the last page.

iUniverse rev. date: 02/08/2019

Foreword

My personal connection to the author is best described as a multitiered portrait of the man himself, in all his various compounded forms. It is rare, in my experience, to find a man so consummately suited for the different roles he plays in his life. As a father, teacher, comedian, businessman, and man of God, he assimilates each responsibility in its totality and executes the charge with acuity and authenticity. I am fortunate to have been acquainted with each personality, at its best.

Every interaction with Eddie B leaves me fascinated by the effortless way he lives a life that has been mercilessly agitated by obstacles and pain. The father in him rises to the occasion fearlessly, with a strength reminiscent of warriors on the field of battle. Eddie has joined the ranks of a growing demographic. A survey of the changing profile of unmarried parents by Pew Research shows that as of April 2018, one in four American parents is unmarried. Of that number, 12 percent of those raising children are single dads. While that number has held steady over the years, it has done so in the face of a lower percentage of households run by single moms. Yet, with the numbers (and some might argue the odds), stacked disproportionately with regard to his acceptance in a society prone to be more sympathetic to the plight of solo moms, his dedication to his son is indefatigable. Even with the rigors that come with providing for a child as an unmarried father, he is a fount of support. Though we are separated by some years, I have benefitted from his wisdom and advice. He's been generous with his time on several occasions. We forged a bond bridged by our paternal predisposition. It is this connectivity that is evident when he steps on to a stage or stands in front of a classroom. He performs, teaches, and relates from the viewpoint of fatherly affection.

Eddie B, the educator, has earned the respect and admiration of the millions who attend his shows. While I know he appreciates the legions of fans who applaud him and watch his videos, I can attest to the fact that ultimately one of his biggest priorities is working with children—the students he teaches and the young men and women he mentors. He is an indefatigable advisor, always willing to sacrifice his time to ensure the next generation will be educated, and socially aware and mentally equipped to take on a world that has proved (time and time again) to be cruel and challenging *but* also hopeful and favorable. It takes an extremely grounded person to strike a balance between life's obstacles and opportunities. Eddie B walks that fine line with precision. All the qualities I have just described are illustrated in the pages of his first book; his poignant observations from a teacher's point of view tell the story of professionals who give so much of their own lives (and sanity) for their pupils.

Watching Eddie teach is a stirring experience. I had the opportunity to observe the man in his academic element and was reminded to never judge a book by its cover. He is much more than meets the eye. The outpouring of passion and dedication, the wealth of knowledge he shares so generously in the classroom, and the patience and understanding that inspires even the most reluctant student are an extraordinary combination that is surpassed only by his talent as a comedian.

Eddie B is the epitome of comic excellence. He performs with focus, intensity, intelligence, and a deep respect for the art of comedy. I discovered, while working with Eddie during the acclaimed tour The 5 Degrees of Comedy, that he is a polished humorist, not a hackneyed wisecracking jokester. Whether he is working as part of a comedy ensemble known for highly educated men with a talent for telling jokes or as a solo artist, he takes performing (and the love of his fans) very seriously.

Comedy is in Eddie's blood; it's part of who he is. Most days, it is difficult to determine where his professional and personal life ends and comedy begins. Consequently, it came as no surprise to me and others that he found a way to fuse his love of teaching with his desire to make people laugh. What you will read in the pages of this book and hopefully one day (for those who have not already) see on stage is his pure devotion to bringing laughter.

Few people are aware that the man with the signature Teachers Only Comedy Tour taking over theaters and arenas across America is also a guy with a divine purpose. He can quote scripture as easily as he can recite Shakespeare. In all he does, Eddie puts God first—even when he is making people laugh. It is the strength of his faith, I imagine, that keeps him grounded and humble. Some people talk about giving it all to God and being grateful for the little things, despite life being fraught with incredible challenges, but Eddie B walks the walk daily. One of the hardest-working men I know, he is not given to whining, complaining, or asking for handouts. He'd rather go hungry than saddle friends and family with his troubles.

What's more, Eddie is consistent. Notoriety and success have not changed him, and I am confident it never will. In fact, both have made him more modest and thoughtful. When all is said and done, he'd rather use his newfound fame to help his fellow teachers, family, and friends. It's part of the reason he wrote this book. Eddie understands God has blessed him with countless gifts, and with his good fortune, he can touch people's lives in positive ways. You, the reader, are one of those persons.

Those who have had the pleasure of meeting Eddie B know he is a stand-up guy. I can personally confirm he is as openhearted and gregarious one-on-one as he is when he's embracing the thousands who attend his shows. I hope everyone will have the opportunity to experience what this young man has to offer. Whether it is in the pages of this book or during one of his performances, to be in his presence is like being touched by a goodness few will ever truly comprehend.

It is my privilege to introduce you to Eddie B: father, teacher, comic, and man of God.

Carlos Wallace,

author of *Life Is Not Complicated—You Are*

My Prince, My Struggle, My Redemption

"THERE IS A THIN LINE that separates laughter and pain, comedy and tragedy, humor and hurt," humorist Erma Bombeck once wrote.

Amen to that. Truer words were never written.

Most comics understand what Ms. Bombeck meant by that statement. Many of us have had to swim against the tide through oceans of challenges before we are finally given an opportunity to sail off into a sunset. Hopefully we are buoyed by waves of laughter and applause. And even then, if you are not prudent (or humble), you will end up barely treading water. Stand-up comics hide a great deal from the world. Behind the jokes and smiling faces typically lies a past full of pain, depression, anxiety, and insecurity. We hide it well.

In order to understand why I am eternally grateful for the success of the Teachers Only tour, I feel I owe it to my supporters to share a part of my journey few people know about. I don't intend to turn this book into some sad account of my struggles, trials, and tribulations. However, you have all given me so much (including sharing your personal stories as a source of encouragement) that it would only be fair to reciprocate. I want to open up briefly about why comedy, my career as a teacher, this tour, and all of you are so important to me. You deserve that much.

The Teachers Only tour has transformed my life. Few words can articulate how much I enjoy being on that stage in front of my colleagues from around the world. It is so rare these days to find men and women, from every walk of life and with varied religious beliefs and different socioeconomic statuses, who can come together and thoroughly appreciate a common cause. No politics, no animus, no judgment. Just pure entertainment. For me, the motivation runs deeper.

I was a young single father fighting for custody of my son. The original motion was for joint custody. I had no idea how things would unfold and no clue as to what arrangement would be made. I do know that I was nervous and scared. I've heard horror stories about fathers having difficulty obtaining custody in Texas. There is a general presumption that joint custody will be most beneficial to the child. That would have sufficed, but after months of legal limbo and testing the edges of patience, a judge awarded me full custody. It happened right around my son's birthday too. It was an ideal outcome on the perfect day.

I walked out of the courtroom on cloud nine. I did not know what obstacles (if any) might lie ahead, but I was convinced my love for my son and my faith in God would guide us the rest of the way.

When reality set in, it was like a punch to the throat. I loved my son, but the responsibility that came with raising him on my own was greater than I expected. I had to dedicate every second of every day to EJ's care. Doctor's visits? On me. Dental appointments? On me. Parent-teacher conferences? On me. Fevers, coughs, tantrums? On me. Homework, breakfast, lunch, and dinner? On me. Childcare? On me. Ironing and washing clothes while giving him as much attention and support as he could handle? All on me. I never complained. But God help me, I was overwhelmed.

We lived in a house that was in desperate need of repair. Exposed pipes, a dilapidated old bathroom, no heat when it was cold, no air-conditioning when it was hot. I used to collect water in a bucket and heat it on the stove so my child could bathe—standing in a plastic bin, looking tiny and fragile. I could not control my tears. I always made sure he was standing with his back to me so he did not see his father cry. My son did not deserve to live like that. His innocence kept him shielded from the full impact of the hardship we were experiencing. He splashed around in that bucket like it was a luxury swimming pool. The house needed repairs I could barely afford, which meant I had to find additional income.

Comedy shows were a valuable source, but to make extra cash I also began doing odd jobs, including selling comedy tickets for a promoter who was a good friend and a mentor. I worked for Uber to bring in more money—until the car I leased from the company got towed. By the way, that happened the same week our personal vehicle got hauled away! Yet through it all, I made sure my son always knew he was loved, wanted, and safe.

I began chronicling my life in journals. As I reread the pages now, I can't help but notice the notes I jotted in the margins: "EJ sitting on my lap," "EJ writing on his pad sitting next to me," "EJ sleeping on my chest as I write this," "EJ asked if I would ever leave him," "EJ holding me so tight I don't want to move." He was and will forever be my little man, my ride or die, my life. Nobody told me it would be this tough, but the love empowered me. Before he fell asleep and I saw the peace in his eyes, it was as if he was saying, "Good job today, Dad. We can start again tomorrow!"

I didn't come from a rich family. Prior to entering college, I lived with my mother and grandmother. Those two women taught me to be a gentleman, a provider, the kind of man a woman would love to marry. I never wanted for love or affection—or tough love when I needed it. My dream was to become a pro football player. They encouraged me every step of the way. My mother nearly went broke buying uniforms and equipment and paying for sports camps. My plan was to pay them back in spades. I was going to sign a multimillion-dollar contract and put my mom and grandmother on easy street. After all their sacrifices, they deserved that and more.

I never got the chance.

My mother and grandmother both passed away within two years of each other. My grandmother died right before my senior year in high school, and my mom succumbed to pancreatic cancer during my freshman year of college. I will never forget the day she called to tell me she had been diagnosed with that dreadful disease. Her words broke my heart: "Marquis"—my middle name—"I'm scared." The sentiment ripped through me like a bullet. She was the strongest woman I'd known. Fear was not in her DNA. That moment, I decided to come home during the next break. *Fuck school, fuck football—my mom comes first.*

I kept my word. When I got to the house, I saw how much weight she had lost and how weak the chemotherapy made her. I nearly lost it. Of course, I had to be strong— for her.

After a week, she asked when I was going back to school. My mother was so proud that I was the first person in our immediate family to attend college. I looked her in the eyes and told her that I wasn't. "I'm going to stay and take care of you." She tried to resist, but that time, Mom did not know best. She finally realized how serious I was and stopped resisting.

Her words remain on my heart: "Son, everything you gave up to take care of me, God is going to give it back to you and more!" I thought nothing of it at the time.

I was nineteen years old when my mother went to be with the Lord. It was just my brother and me. We were inconsolable, but we had to man up. My mother raised men who persevered and not boys who gave up.

Not a day goes by when I do not think of my mother and grandmother. There is a void in my soul that will never be filled. EJ has managed to fill every bit of my heart, but nothing, no one, can replace a mother's love. I know she and my grandmother are with me always, guiding me and watching over my son. The thought of those two angels looking down empowers me and forces me to do better.

Comedy has given me a new chance at happiness. When I walk through the crowd and embrace the fans and talk to my fellow educators at a show, I am energized. Every appearance, every autograph, every joke, every performance comes from a grateful heart.

If you happen to notice a light radiating from my smile, that's my momma letting me know she's proud and my grandmother reminding me to stay humble. Both make sure I always keep God close.

My life is not perfect, but it's good. Thank God.

Teaching Was Becoming a Health Hazard

MY RELATIONSHIP WITH TEACHING WAS volatile. Some days I hated it. Other days, I loved it. Most times, the profession was very kind to me. Aside from being a source of income that allowed me to provide for my family, teaching gave me a sense of fulfilment. I felt like I was making a difference in the lives of children and somehow contributing to the future of society. Sometimes though, things got rocky. The culture, the work, the bureaucracy, and the stress often caused me to reevaluate my decision to become an educator. I walked a thin line between inspiration and despair. It was a lot like my love life at the time. I dated women with superb qualities, but a few of them had serious personal issues that often upset the balance of our union. Basically, they were insane. I never knew what I was going to get.

Admittedly, when it was good, it was fantastic. Therefore, each new school year, when I agreed to give my relationship with academia another try, I rolled the dice and prayed we would not break up.

One back-to-school season in particular stands out. I remember it like it was yesterday. I was looking forward to the upcoming academic year because I finally had a firm grasp on the sixth-grade science curriculum. I was definitely on more stable ground and eager to apply a ton of new ideas into my lesson plans and take my labs to another level. I thought, *This could potentially become a lifelong career.* My friends could hardly believe this change of heart. *Eddie Brown actually enjoyed teaching? Awesome!*

Everything was falling into place. What could go wrong?

Famous last words. My relationship with teaching was about to hit a rough patch.

The news was not good. Massive job cuts were being discussed within the Houston Independent School District. The Houston Federation of Teachers estimated that deep budget cuts could mean as many as seven hundred positions would be slashed. The school district's board of trustees approved an unspecified reduction of force for teachers and other campus-based employees. Among the positions on the chopping block: secondary math, science, and English. Bilingual education and some special education were exempt from the cuts.

That science part, of course, concerned me the most. I had been at the school for three years. As far as standardized test scores were concerned, my class ranked among the lowest-performing groups. Despite my best efforts, my students lagged behind the national average. If they were looking for someone to cut from the team, I would be in the crosshairs. Keep in mind, I was a single father on a fixed income who was trying to build a comedy career. A pink slip would clash with my plans.

Rarely do teachers look forward to the first meeting of the school year. In fact, we seldom look forward to any meetings. That year, we could not get to the auditorium fast enough. The threat of losing your job makes one very diligent. The principal stepped up to the podium, and we could tell the situation was grave. His words cut deep. It was not the typical explanation of old standards and norms for the year. He did not mention the standard "new focus initiative" in his remarks. Instead, he informed us that the district was implementing a revised appraisal system. *Oh boy.* The upgrade was intended to govern the effectiveness of teachers. *Here we go.* Bottom line, the district was downsizing and closing schools—and he couldn't guarantee everyone's job security. *That's reassuring.*

The buzz of murmurs, heavy sighs, and heated criticism of the principal's comments began as soon as he stopped speaking. We all felt helpless. The appraisal he talked about set us up for failure. The way it was designed made it nearly impossible to receive a perfect evaluation, which further threatened our job security. I felt it was the district's way of strategically phasing out a certain demographic of teachers. I left that meeting with more questions than answers. My stress level was in the red.

I was still performing in the evenings. Thankfully, supportive family members were willing to babysit my son while I chased my dream of being a full-time stand-up comic. I was filling in as a host at "The Horn," a popular club (which has since closed) on the Richmond Strip(in Houston TX) that was one of the hottest open mics at the time. The unlimited supply of free drinks made that gig even more enjoyable. The first cocktail calmed my nerves.

I still got nervous before hitting the stage, but I respected the art and did not take the mic (or the audience's reaction) for granted. The next three or four glasses of liquid courage took the edge off and helped me maintain that relaxed feeling. The stage and those drinks were my escape from the rigors of the classroom. I enjoyed every minute of it.

I'd arrive at work, functioning on fumes. I was getting about two or three hours of sleep a night. Why should I dedicate myself to my day job? After the meeting with the principal, it was clear that the district couldn't care less about any innovative ideas I brought to the table, especially if they did not align with their researched trainings. Teaching, once again, became nothing more than a living wage.

I was miserable. And agitated. And anxious. My nerves were fried. With budget cuts looming, I didn't know when the other shoe would drop.

One morning, I woke up feeling under the weather. I glanced over at my girlfriend, and she was still fast asleep. I went into the bathroom to wash my face and brush my teeth. Something was just not right. The right side of my face felt numb. *Did I sleep in an awkward position? Had I somehow applied too much pressure to my face?* I was up, but my face was still asleep. I continued with my morning routine and got my son ready for school. Thirty minutes after I noticed the lethargy in my face, I pointed it out to my girlfriend. She laughed at first because I had a habit of joking, and she did not realize I was serious. She comforted me and told me the feeling would likely improve as the day progressed.

It did not. I started freaking out. Surely, I was too young to be having a stroke. I did what most normal, paranoid people do in these circumstances: I self-diagnosed. I began googling the symptoms and combing through WebMD articles as if I was doing research for a dissertation. I masked my concern because I did not want to upset my students. By the time school let out, the situation had not improved. *What is going on with me?*

That night, I went to the emergency room for a professional diagnosis. WebMD had me dying of everything from an aneurism to eye cancer. After an examination that included a CT scan, the doctor returned and said, "Good news. You are not having a stroke."

Well, that's a relief.

He told me I had developed a nervous condition called Bell's palsy, a type of facial paralysis that results in an inability to control the facial muscles on the affected side. The leading cause of the condition was stress.

Shocker. Of course I was stressed. People were getting fired all around me, and I did not know if I would be next. The doctor prescribed some steroids and nerve medication that I would have to take for a little over a week. He explained that the only effective treatment was staying hydrated, getting plenty of rest, and time. His prognosis was reassuring. Improvement would be gradual, but recovery times varied from person to person. I should begin to get better within two weeks, and I would probably recover completely, returning to normal function within three to six months.

I was able to take a few sick days. Emphasis on a *few.* Apparently, I was not eligible for supplemental sick leave (short or long-term disability benefits), and the district warned that if I took additional days off, I would be in violation.

Violation? Not eligible? My face was losing the battle with gravity. I went from "Good morning, Mr. Brown" to "What's up, Professor Dead Face?" The medication wore off, but the condition persisted. I was one of few people for whom the symptoms lasted longer. I also faced the possibility that the disorder might never disappear completely. Even if it did, in rare cases, the palsy may reoccur. However, the bureaucrats in charge—the ones who "cared so much" about my well-being for about five minutes—insisted I get back to work immediately. I was floored at the level of callousness.

It was then and there that I made the conscious decision to never let teaching stress me again. *Chalk this one up to experience.*

It took me five months to recover, but the right side of my face never returned to full functionality. I still feel some tightness, especially if I start to worry too much.

It was a jarring wake-up call that I will never forget. It also gave me the encouragement I needed to pursue my comedy career even more aggressively. Fool me once, shame on you. Fool me twice—well, you know the rest.

Enough

I'D BEEN IN CLASS FOR a total of two hours, but it seemed like it had been days. The kids were taking a test. Except for the occasional heavy sigh, nervous shifting, or shuffle of papers, it was silence.

Suddenly, I became acutely aware of another sound. The persistent, rhythmic, measured, and ridiculously annoying noise coming from an old clock on the wall. I glanced up at the mechanism that, in a matter of minutes, had become my nemesis.

Tick …

Are you serious? Tock …

I'm about to lose it.

Tick …

This is too much. Tock …

You know what? I have had enough!

And with that, I began plotting my escape. I started to think about how I would extract myself from what had become the most agonizing of career choices: teaching. Some days I could barely compel myself to get out of bed, much less muster enough energy to shower, shave, dress, and drive to the school that was the bane of my existence. I don't know when it happened, but somewhere between the hours of study, the mounds of student debt, the first day as a teacher, and my current state of complete apathy, I stopped loving what I did. And despite my best efforts, it showed. My obvious disdain for a career considered among the nobler professions had become so apparent that even my students wondered why I even bothered coming to class.

"Damn, Mr. Brown. You never look happy."

"Um, would you be happy if you had to spend eight hours with you?"

I probably should have exercised more tact, but I no longer cared about being here, about teaching, or about schools. Fortunately, I still loved the kids (well, some of them). I still respected my colleagues and all the hard work they put in day in, day out; they were underappreciated, underpaid, and overworked. I knew I had to get out before I lost sight of the fundamental reason I chose that career. No matter how fed up I was with the system and the everyday grind, I refused to become completely cynical.

For years, I had been waiting for a sign telling me that today is the day you walk away. It could come from God, a principal, the board of education, the lunchroom lady, or that janitor working five years past his retirement. I needed a concrete reason to bail, and quite frankly, I did not much care from where my omen would emerge. Now, being a man given to dramatic flair, I thought my epiphany would manifest in legendary fashion: a story that rivaled the parting of the red sea, the creation of man, or Kanye West's latest breakdown. My awakening was going to be epic, the stuff of legends.

Nope. A clock. It's not the bombshell wave of clarity I was expecting. Funny how the simplest things convince you to reevaluate your entire life. As I sat in my classroom, contemplating my future, looking out at the confused faces staring down at the quiz I know they did not prepare for (despite a week of lead time and being given the answers), listening to the tick, tock, tick, tock, my mind raced. Initially, I wondered how much time I would get for shooting that damn clock. I mean, seriously, if I were not an educated man and somewhat in my right mind, I'd think it was taunting me. The repetitive, predictable, irritating sound was a reflection of my mundane life. Each tick, tock, tick tock reminded me: You … ain't … getting … nowhere.

The clock was my breakthrough. You know you have surpassed your limit when a ticking clock forces you to contemplate homicidal thoughts. God help me.

I often asked myself if I would know when I'd had enough. When the interminable hours in a hot, musty classroom, the never-ending, underappreciated lesson plans, the awkward parent-teacher conferences, the pretending to care about these badass kids when what I really wanted to do was choke-slam the next young miscreant who tested my patience (and Christianity) would eventually take their toll on my good nature.

At first, I thought I was going through a midlife crisis. Actually, let me be honest. I *prayed* to Psychotherapy Jesus that I was having a midlife crisis. At least that would be a decent way to sum up why I was feeling so despondent. When it hit me, I thought, *I don't want to be here today—in this school, with these kids.* Hell, I wasn't halfway through the day before I reminded myself that I didn't even feel like going to that purgatory yesterday. I was stockpiling sick days, keeping a reserve for when I absolutely needed a break and couldn't take it anymore.

I had lesson plans due, goals for each student to set up, kids going in and out of my class all semester, and new evaluation systems in place, which stressed me even more. The people I worked for still had the nerve to talk behind my back, murmuring and complaining about what I was *not* doing. I just held my tongue. They had no clue about what I really wanted to say to—and about—every one of them. Even the morning bell gave me a post-traumatic stress reaction. It reminded me that I was back there in that place. Surely, it was a test of my faith.

The principal walked up to me and asked how I was doing.

I responded, "I am quite grand."

Really? I don't even talk like that! It is proof positive that, in order to be a teacher, you need some serious acting chops. Every day, I had to act like I cared, like I didn't mind going to unnecessary meetings, and like I didn't wish I was anywhere but there.

Lord help me.

To make matters worse, that wasn't even my first choice. Teaching was not even a blip on the radar of my dreams. I wanted to play football. *That* was plan A. Plan B? I wanted to be a physical therapist. If that did not pan out, I would have executed plan C: coaching football and basketball. Basically, teaching wasn't even a part of my ABCs.

Thank God for the stage. Comedy was my release, my therapy. It was a place where I could release my anger and frustration, but it was hard to create time for it when I was committed (by default) to everything that went along with being a teacher, which made me angry and frustrated.

Watch Your Mouth!

WATCH YOUR MOUTH! THIS IS not just a stern warning by "Big Momma" to precocious children on the verge of spouting an inappropriate comment or, even worse, who already flippantly put their feet in their mouths. For me, that is typically what comes to mind when I hear the ominous caveat that has the power to stop kids dead in their tracks, especially when issued by a person whose authority was unquestionable (and who was particularly dexterous with a switch). Most of us have probably said it at least once during the course of a heated argument or debate. I have even advised a few folks to tread lightly with their words lest they cross a dangerous line. Don't get me wrong: disagreements are fine, but a difference of opinion does not give anyone a license to breach the boundaries of respect.

I learned the term "watch your mouth" has another, deeper meaning. Saying whatever is on your mind with reckless abandon is potentially offensive and can alter the course of someone's thinking. When people bombard you with judgment and negative observations, it can ruin your day, alter your mood, and distract you. Who needs people like that in their presence? Imagine if the person putting hostility out in the universe is you!

We've all been there. We get angry, blow off steam, and become eager to get something "off our chest" or "keep it real." Well, as it turns out, nine times out of ten, the only thing we are getting off our chests is uncontrolled emotion, and the only thing we are keeping real is our stress levels. We are keeping them *really* high! In the end, we lay the framework for a mind-set that is fraught with toxic reasoning. It's unhealthy and can lead to unhappiness and depression. The words you proclaim to other people have immense power.

I say "watch your mouth" because I understand what we speak is assimilated into our spirit and directly impacts us. The messages, thoughts, and desires you feed your brain determine your temperament and dictate your frame of mind. While you may derive some temporary satisfaction from disparaging and gossiping about others, the practice blinds you to the fact that those words linger. The sentiment may hurt the intended party, but you have to live with the consequences. Negativity and the dark cloud it casts have permeated your thought process. The only way to recover is to modify your approach. Start putting favorable vibes into the air.

About six years ago, I read a book that transformed my way of thinking. *The Secret* explained how your thoughts define the kind of life you will lead. If you think a certain way, what you envisage will manifest in your daily activities. The book used examples of historical figures who claim they channeled their thoughts into energy. The book's author outlines a three-step process: ask, believe, and receive. I appreciate the biblical reference from Matthew 21:22: "And all things, whatsoever ye shall ask in prayer, believing, ye shall receive."

As a science teacher, I completely grasped the idea explored in *The Secret* as it relates to the law of conservation of energy, which states in part that energy can neither be created nor destroyed. Instead, it transforms or is transferred from one form to another. Basically, the energy we put in the atmosphere stays there and takes form. The same vibration rewards us or teaches us a lesson when it returns to the source: the person who emitted it.

The book planted the seed, but I didn't really begin practicing what I had read until I purchased a car. The vehicle came equipped with free XM radio for three months. I did not have the disposable income to splurge on such luxuries. I was living on a teacher's salary.

One day, I discovered Pastor Joel Osteen's channel. Osteen, founder and leader of Houston's Lakewood Church, preached messages of prosperity, happiness, wealth, health, and peace. He talked about not giving any power to negative thoughts or people. He stressed the importance of faith and prayer. He told stories about people who experienced tragedy and loss and lived with pain and hardship but never succumbed to the challenges. Because of that, God granted them favor. His sermons became as much a part of my morning as taking a shower or eating breakfast. Every single day, when I started my car, it would already be set to Joel's channel. I listened intently, took in every word, and filed away each message for months.

I began not only taking in all the encouraging messages but speaking them into my own being. I did not engage in negativity. I became more optimistic. I acknowledged the incredible things that were happening around me, and I was always thankful for the blessings. When I faced a challenge, I did not let it bring me down or break my spirit. Instead, I focused on the good—the abundance—I knew was in store. I told myself I was rich, I was anointed, and I was worthy.

I sometimes felt so silly sitting in my car or in my classroom ruminating about my "riches" when I knew full well that the district would never allow it. I felt even more foolish declaring how happy I was when my job sickened me or affirming that great things were looming ahead when my goals seemed to be moonwalking in the opposite direction.

My words didn't trigger things immediately. As I began to articulate them, I could feel a shift. I couldn't quite put my finger on when, but I could feel the positive motivation coming back to reward me for being consistent with my upbeat disposition. I never lost hope. Hope is the glue that binds you to your sanguine sensibilities. When you exude gratitude in all you say, you find peace. Your belief is magnified through your testimony. Faith will sustain you through the rough times until the shift becomes reality.

My existence changed in a heartbeat. Everything I uttered helped mold my destiny. The energy boomeranged! I know my good fortune began when I instilled brighter outlooks into horrible situations.

God's grace sustained me through "issue-ations" until it was the right time: my time. This philosophy transcends teaching, educators, and students. It affects the well-being of all people—no matter their religion, race, or social standing.

Your words will dictate your progress. I challenge anyone reading this chapter to start watching what you say; I guarantee your life will change for the better.

Meeting the Secretary
of Education

THE TEACHERS ONLY COMEDY TOUR changed my life. I went from performing on local stages in Houston (in front of ten, thirty, up to three hundred people), to telling jokes in major arenas and theaters across the country. Tens of thousands of supportive fans—teachers with whom I share a unique bond—welcomed me with open arms, loud cheers, and contagious laughter.

From Charlotte to New York City, Dallas to Biloxi, Baton Rouge to Seattle, Montgomery to Denver, and countless other cities across America, my gratitude knows no bounds.

I still cannot believe how drastically my life transformed after releasing the first video. I was at the end of my rope, twisting in the wind. I worried about caring for my son and paying my bills. I was depressed and fearful, but as God is my witness, I never lost faith. I prayed every day and waited for an answer. The blessings were bestowed in abundance. The best gift? To be able to care for my family while doing something I loved (performing and teaching).

I am living proof that God never forsakes us.

The comedy shows and the *What Teachers Really Say* videos also began opening doors I never dreamed possible. I was offered opportunities to speak up for the men and women who dedicate their lives to teaching. Forty shows and seventy videos into a new phase of my life, a major development occurred.

The Teachers Only Comedy Tour took our crew to Washington DC. I had never been to the nation's capital, so I was very excited about performing there. When I arrived, I headed straight to the hotel to rest before the show. The agency that represented me at the time had a habit of checking on me via text or phone call each time I arrived at any destination, so I was not surprised when they reached out to me that morning. The rep on the other end sounded excited and a little apprehensive. All I wanted was to get some sleep, and I quietly wished he would just come out and tell me what had him bouncing off the walls.

After a minute of small talk, he informed me that word of the tour had reached officials in DC—and the secretary of education, Betsy DeVos, wanted to meet with me.

I damn near lost consciousness. Actually, I may have lost consciousness for a few seconds. I definitely hyperventilated for a couple minutes. Suffice it to say, I was not the personification of calm, cool, or collected.

My reaction shifted from "kid at Christmas" to confused as hell. Why on earth would a government official want to meet with me? I was just a tired, overworked teacher— not unlike any other public school educator (working or retired). I was speaking out through my comedy, but so many before me had spoken up as well. I was perplexed. What made me special?

Oh well, no time for introspection.

First step: The agency needed to look into the request further. They wanted a more comprehensive explanation as to why I was being summoned. Okay, "summoned" may be a bit intense, but I am trying to give you a sense of how dramatically it was playing out in my head. Bottom line, my circle wanted to ensure it was not some gratuitous publicity stunt. I had become well-known to educators, and they did not want public officials taking advantage of my newfound popularity.

Second step: Get input from my teacher community. I posted an update about the impromptu invitation on my social media platforms, and it did not take long for the comments to add up. Some encouraged me to meet with Secretary DeVos. It was the chance of a lifetime—a perfect opportunity to give her a piece of our collective minds as a spokesperson for all teachers. Others warned me to steer clear of Madam Secretary and the Department of Education building, joking I was being set up and walking into an ambush, complete with snipers on the roof ready to take me out as soon as I stepped out of the Uber: "Remember what happened to Martin and Malcolm! Folks don't like it when you start speaking the truth!"

Apparently, I have quite a few militants on my page.

The feedback was all in good fun though, and everyone meant well. That really helped settle my nerves and let me wrap my brain around the importance of what was happening. I (like many of my fellow teachers) am so passionate about making a difference in the lives of the children we teach. If meeting Mrs. DeVos could in any way set the stage for constructive, productive dialogue between educators and the government agency that establishes policy for—and administers and coordinates most federal assistance to—education, it would be a major step toward giving our country's kids a better chance to succeed.

It did not take long for the agency to approve the meeting. Obviously, I had already passed the required background checks; otherwise, the invite would not have been extended. With everyone on board, I got dressed (I had to look sharp), splashed on some cologne, and freshened my breath. I could not show up funky. That would not be a good look. I was definitely trying to make the best impression. I met up with team, and we were on our way.

The Department of Education headquarters is located inside the Lyndon Baines Johnson building, which is about fifty-seven years old. The federal edifice looks like most of the government dwellings on that campus, not very modern and designed for functionality. I did a quick sniper check. All good.

I walked into the DoED building and was immediately fascinated by its stark, businesslike tone. It smelled like bureaucracy: cold, detached, and stifling. Our escort was not very chatty. I wanted to crack some jokes to loosen him up, but then I thought better of it. Nothing about the office suggested a sense of humor.

As I followed the serious-looking gentleman down a maze of corridors and through metal detectors, I began to feel like I'd been called to the principal's office. I felt like I was walking the long mile to learn my fate, and I was still not sure if I was in trouble or not. I did know there were way too many American flags and DoEd logos lining the hallways for me not to take several selfies when it was over. Several.

Admittedly, it felt good to be in the building where decisions that affect education are made. When teachers pray for reform in the country's school systems and plead that someone in a position to make changes takes time to understand our needs, that building would be where you want those appeals to be heard. I was inside the "Education Mothership."

We sat in a huge waiting room for about ten minutes, talking among ourselves. We were a group of regular people on a comedy tour, and we had to try hard to behave ourselves and resist the urge to cut up. Everyone was doing their best to keep me calm. I was grateful for my team.

A young woman entered the room—I assumed she was an aide—and said, "Okay, everyone, follow me please."

She led us to one of the biggest offices I have ever seen. As I walked in, I heard my mom's voice in my head: "Boy, you better act like you been somewhere before!" My momma was always with me. I know she was beaming with pride looking down at her baby boy as he stood in Betsy DeVos's office.

Moments later, the Secretary of Education walked in. I greeted her politely and quickly introduced her to everyone in our group. My mouth was saying, "It is such a pleasure to meet you, Madam Secretary." My inner monologue was screaming, *Damn, you look very well-off, ma'am. Very wealthy. What I'm sayin' is, you look like money, ma'am!*

I had to keep joking to myself to keep from losing it.

Mrs. DeVos greeted me warmly and thanked me for coming. Her assistant, who stood by at a comfortable distance, asked us all to be seated. Secretary DeVos wasted no time getting the conversation started. "So, Eddie, if you had a magic wand, what would you change about education?"

I thought, *Man, you better not mess this up! Teachers everywhere are counting on you.*

The floor was mine.

As I talked about the concerns of our profession and outlined my suggestions for improving how teachers are treated, which would ultimately help us better serve the needs of our students, she listened intently. I believed she was genuinely interested in hearing what was on my mind and considered me a credible spokesperson for teachers around the nation. I thought about all the emails I had received, the teary-eyed teachers who confided in me at my shows, and the protests I watched on television and participated in as teachers begged for fair wages and a better quality of life. I thought about every time we had to spend our own money to buy school supplies and decorate our classrooms. I remembered every night my son fell asleep on my lap as I graded papers or wrote up lesson plans. Those thoughts flooded my brain and poured out of me as I explained the plight of those I proudly represented: the tired, worn, overworked, underpaid, and underappreciated educators.

I shifted into teaching mode. For thirty-five minutes, I stood in front of this "class" and presented the most important lesson of my career. I explained why we deserved higher salaries and smaller class sizes and why the system had to do away with unfair standardized testing. I provided specific data and details, and I shared personal experiences to support my claims.

As I spoke, she listened and nodded. Sometimes she looked shocked. When I joked, she smiled. When she noticed that some of my concerns were painful to express, she appeared concerned.

The assistant diligently documented the exchange.

When I was done, Mrs. DeVos stood up, smiled broadly, shook my hand for a very long time, looked me in my eyes, and thanked me.

My heart overflowed. I was humbled by the accomplishment. Maybe she heard and understood everything I said—or maybe it went in one ear and out the other. I know teachers everywhere would have given anything for a chance to talk to their administrators or directors the way I spoke to Mrs. DeVos that day, expressing themselves without fear of retaliation, being depicted in a negative light, strategically moved out of the district, or labeled as a troublemaker.

I do not know exactly what will come of that meeting, but I want my fellow educators to know I believe I represented us well. I did the best I could to ensure—in that room, at that moment—that our voices were not silenced. We were not agitators or complainers. We were respected members of the teaching community, and our concerns were heard. Changes will come eventually, and I hope to be in more positions to play an instrumental role in that progress.

That night, after such a momentous experience, I spent an evening with the people I appreciate the most, doing what I love to do. I performed in front of a standing room-only crowd of the most amazing people: my fellow teachers and their friends and families.

Yeah, that was a great day indeed.

What's in a Name?

Let's clear up some misconceptions, shall we?

The occupation of "teacher," as defined by Wikipedia:

> A teacher (also called a school teacher or, in some contexts, an educator) is a person who helps others to acquire knowledge, competences or values. Informally the role of teacher may be taken on by anyone (e.g. when showing a colleague how to perform a specific task). In some countries, teaching young people of school age may be carried out in an informal setting, such as within the family (homeschooling), rather than in a formal setting such as a school or college.

If only it were that simple.

I often wonder what people who do not work in academia think teachers do all day. I mean, I want to know what they *really* think. Judging by the total lack of interest most folks show when the topic of teachers comes up in the news or in general conversation about the workforce—not to mention the complete disregard for the difficulties public school teachers encounter each time they set foot on campus—I can say with 100 percent certainty that a lot of people do not have a clue about what we endure.

Our lives and daily activities—in fact, our entire profession—are encapsulated (mistakenly) within the definition or some variation of the top of this chapter. Basically, the supposition is we come to school, walk into a classroom, teach a subject for about four hours, break for lunch, return to the classroom, teach for another three hours or so, and go home once the students are dismissed. If this is indeed the presumption, then I can't blame the general public for being apathetic. Hell, I'd be mad too if a bunch of people with such an easy job were constantly complaining about the daily grind, lack of respect, low pay, limited resources, heavy workload, overflowing classrooms, and unruly students. The nerve!

But I know better.

Bear with me. This is not a rant, tantrum, or pointless tirade. If the Teachers Only tour and the *What Teachers Really Say* videos have done anything, they have given me a platform to finally enlighten the nation about the rigors of the profession we sacrifice so much to be a part of. Most days, I do it with humor. I want to take a moment, however, to explain why our jobs are so important to us.

Teachers are overworked, underpaid, and underappreciated. This is not to suggest other jobs do not possess distinct challenges. However, I can only attest to my own experience. Quite frankly, few jobs have the added obligation of shaping the minds of children who are not our own, disciplining children who are not our own, and mentoring, counseling, comforting, encouraging, and caring for children who are not our own—all because we want to make a difference. We know we are not going to get rich. We acknowledge there is nothing glamorous about lesson plans, out-of-date textbooks, checking homework, grading tests and papers, and field trips on the coldest or hottest day of the year. Nevertheless, we wake up each day with one mission: to do everything in our power to prepare children for a better future.

Teacher salaries are such a joke that our paychecks could get on a stage and do a comedy set. The average pay is on par with (barely) or drastically less than a number of occupations that don't even require much education. According to Payscale.com, the average earnings of workers with at least a four-year college degree are more than 50 percent higher than teachers' average earnings. If you place the salaries of teachers with graduate degrees alongside that of other professionals, the figures are even more alarming: education jobs scraped the bottom across the board. Among greater Houston's larger school districts, HISD teachers rank among the lowest paid when comparing educators of the same experience levels.

And while most non-salaried employees can rack up overtime, the website shows that teachers work an average of fifty-three hours per week. The thirteen hours we work in addition to the forty hours we sign up for? Unpaid labor. And that "summer vacation" people love to throw in our faces? We are not compensated for those days.

Wait, there's more. Given the workload we shoulder throughout the school year, we have to perform many of our duties (grading papers, preparing lesson plans and assignments) after school, on weekends, or whenever we have "free time." Therefore, it is very difficult for teachers to take the regular vacation days we are allotted. Imagine having families, friends, and outside interests—and having little to zero time to dedicate to any of that because you are literally working year-round.

Oh, and did I mention that many teachers are forced to get second, or even third, jobs to supplement their teaching salaries? The fact that we show up, every day, despite everything we deal with should be reason enough to earn consistent raises and competitive salaries.

Still, amid a decline in student enrollment (especially in Houston), proposed budget cuts, and stagnant salaries, we are expected to work miracles. The powers that be want us to prepare kids who possess varied levels of intellectual ability for standardized tests. Doesn't "standard" suggest the exams should apply to students across the board? Subjecting a class that is all over the map when it comes to comprehension, retention, and learning to a boilerplate test is unfair.

The people setting the guidelines have (more than likely) never set foot inside a classroom and do not have the faintest idea what teachers on the front line actually deal with. That is a major drawback. Classroom management is the foundation of the profession. Unless you have executed a lesson plan while kids with short attention spans are running around the classroom, you cannot relate. If you have not had the responsibility of running a classroom where many of the students cannot speak English, behave as if they should be medicated (or are off their meds), or read at levels lower than the grade they are in, you are not qualified to suggest procedures. If you have not juggled responsibilities like an educational acrobat and were still required to honor unfair mandates and paperwork that do not have any bearing on the outcome of the students' schooling, you are unqualified to dictate protocol. Participating in day-to-day classroom routines for at least five years should be a prerequisite for anyone seeking an administrative position. Think of it as a boot camp for bosses.

Having said all this, I find it interesting that our voices only get heard if we beat the drum, sound the alarm, and blare the air horn of our discontent during protests or walkouts. We have to resort to vociferous extremes in order to make our complaints known. It's shameful and disheartening. In the end, we do what we have to in order to get what we need.

A teacher's most important charge is to make an impact on our students and ensure they become productive, successful citizens. Almost every success story includes a chapter that recognizes the positive influence of an educator. That is a testament to the fact a teacher's passion is powerful enough to change the world.

I am honored to be among an army of game changers who consistently power the world. Keep up the great work!

What Teachers Really Say

THERE ARE FEW SOUNDS LOUDER (or as humiliating) than a tow truck outside your window at seven o'clock in the morning.

I didn't even have to wonder whose car was getting hooked up. The way my luck had been going lately, as soon as I heard the truck idling and its gears grinding, I knew it was going to be another bad day in what was turning into a series of dark, bleak weeks. Man, why do they choose to completely wreck your day at the crack of dawn? I walked outside my house just as the driver was attaching the chain to my car. He stood there, cigarette dangling from his lip, watching the front end of the car rising slowly off the ground. My neighbors had gathered around to observe the display. You would have thought it was the season finale of their favorite Netflix series. Someone pulled out their camera phone and began recording the scene. The sun wasn't even hot yet, and those folks were already fired up, wide-awake, and feeling petty. I guess nothing says, "I'm better than you" than wallowing in another person's misery.

As I walked toward my car, I made eye contact with the tow truck operator. Part of me was hoping he would see the desperation on my face and be moved by some sense of man-to-man, brothers-in-the-struggle feeling and take pity on me. No such luck. His face was borderline expressionless. I searched for a hint of compassion. Then, almost imperceptible at first but becoming unmistakable, a smile: the dude was smiling. The devil was busy and working for a tow truck company! I wanted to slap that smug look off his face, but he was a big guy. Massive. And since he was in the process of taking legal possession of my property, I was not in any credible position to flex on him—or anybody else for that matter.

I swallowed my pride, which went down like broken glass, and walked back into the house. I had to find a way to get to work. It was not the best way to start the day.

Something had to give—soon.

That would be my last year as a teacher—at least that's what I kept telling myself. Honestly, I'd been saying that for years. I started to doubt I'd ever break free of the classroom chaos that wreaked havoc on my mental and physical health. Teaching is arguably one of the most noble professions. It is also the most stressful, thankless, tiring, and draining jobs on the face of the earth. I had checked out a long time ago. Comedy had become my job, and I was just using teaching to pay the bills. I needed that steady paycheck to subsist. Paying for flights to and from out-of-town gigs and investing in marketing and promotion campaigns was not cheap. I had to suck it up. I prayed every day for God to give me strength and order my steps (and keep me from putting one of these people's kids in a choke hold).

I managed to get to work on time. My son was with me, but walking into the building was traumatic. I felt my chest tighten and my temples throb. I broke out in a cold sweat, and my fingers clenched into fists. Why was I so angry? It was not normal! I could feel EJ looking up at me, aware something was not right. I stepped into the men's room, and he stood at the door, wide-eyed. I tried to steady my breathing. I splashed cold water on my face and hovered over the sink for a few minutes as the water trickled down my face and into my collar. I lifted my head slowly and looked into the mirror. The man looking back at me was a stranger. I think at one point he wanted to play football and make enough money to shower his mom and grandmother with beautiful homes and fancy cars. That may have been the guy who planned on giving his son the world—the life he never had. That guy used to be confident and in control. I stared at that man for what seemed an eternity. I didn't blink. I barely breathed. And then, he said, "God has a different plan. Be patient."

The man in the bathroom mirror just gave me advice? I am officially losing it.

I grabbed EJ's hand, and we walked to my classroom. I set my briefcase down and sat at my desk. I looked around at the empty seats and began thinking about all the things I disliked about teaching. Suddenly, my brain was on fire. Ideas started forming, taking shape, and making sense. I had begun producing videos where I would play different characters: Jealous Guy, El Puncho the Boxer, Preacher Man. I received positive feedback, but it was not nearly as much as I needed to make a dent on social media. Let's face it, five thousand views, while respectable, was just not going to cut it. On Instagram, YouTube, and Facebook, comics were racking up millions of views daily.

As you may know by now, I am a prayerful man. I asked God to help me formulate a great idea, something I had never done before. It actually felt weird, praying for comic inspiration, but I was desperate and did not care if my requests to our Lord and Savior were cool or appropriate. I needed divine intervention. If it came in the form of a multimillion-dollar concept, I wouldn't be mad.

Out of nowhere, it dawned on me. Why not make a video about teaching? I felt kind of stupid for not thinking about it before, but God works on His own time. I, on the other hand, did not have that luxury. These kids were going to start coming through the door any minute, and I had to get my act together! I explained to my son why he needed to keep quiet while I was recording. Basically, I bribed him with a promise of ice cream later that afternoon. Don't judge me.

Suffice it to say, I was not technologically prepared for my moment of inspiration. I did not have a fancy phone, a tripod, or a selfie stick. Who expects they are going to get all Martin Scorsese during first period? I set the phone on the computer cart next to my desk. The biggest challenge was making sure I was centered in the shot. I only had a few minutes to get it right. Fortunately, it was not hard to come up with material. I'd been an educator for some time.

The crazy experiences began flooding my senses. The spontaneous performance began as a rant. If it bothered me as a teacher, I talked about it. The good, the bad, and the ugly. Classroom chronicles, teacher tantrums, student shenanigans, district drama, bureaucratic bull … well, you know what I mean. I had so many memories stored up that filling the time was effortless. When my tirade finally ended, I had recorded so much footage it was nearly impossible to trim it all down to one minute. Still, I was ecstatic. Finally, I had something about the job I could find some pleasure in.

That was a short-lived feeling. I could hear them before I could see them. The students began to line up outside my classroom door, but the video was all I could think of. I needed to edit the clip before the end of the school day.

I assigned the dream killers (yes, at that moment, that is precisely what they were) some "busy work." It was just enough to keep them occupied throughout the period. I locked the door because I did not want to risk an administrator sticking their head in and taking note of what I was doing. There really was no valid reason for me to be on my cell phone while class was in session.

I worked frantically. I'm pretty sure the kids thought I was crazy because I kept smiling and laughing at some of the comments in the video. By the time the lunch bell rang, I was almost done editing. After quickly escorting my students to the cafeteria, I damn near ran back to my room to finish up. Since I had a few minutes, I decided to include a few shots of me in front of my smart board to give the finished product a little creativity. The entire process was cathartic. It felt good to get all those thoughts off my chest.

Next big problem: I didn't have a clue what to title the video, and I did not have a lot of time to ponder it. The kids would be back soon, and I had to at least act like I was there to teach them something. That was it! I was a teacher—and it was what I really want to say. I named it "What Teachers Really Say This Time of Year."

The video ran about one minute, which allowed me to share it on Instagram that afternoon. Later on, I uploaded the clip to Facebook. I was so proud of myself. The sense of accomplishment was indescribable. By the end of the work day, I had amassed about four thousand views per video. It was pretty typical for me.

That evening, EJ and I got home pretty late. I glanced over at the empty spot in the driveway where our car used to be. Reality check. I didn't dwell. I had to prepare for a science lab the next day, and I got right to work. It never dawned on me to check the progress of my latest video. Quite frankly, I thought the views had maxed out that afternoon. Besides, it had been a long day, and my bed was calling. I laid down and thought about the "What Teachers Really Say" concept. I didn't know how far I could take it, but I was definitely willing to explore producing a series of them, if for no other reason, than to vent about life as a teacher in a humorous way. I finally dozed off.

The alarm clock blared the next morning. How long had I been asleep? Not long enough. Note to self: get rid of that obnoxious clock. Damn near gave me a heart attack. I reached for my phone and opened up the Facebook app. I could not believe what I saw. I sat up, put the phone down, rubbed my eyes, and picked up the phone again. No, I was not imagining it. The video was up to 100,000 views. What's more, the comments from teachers around the world were pouring in. Educators were sharing their thoughts about the video and remarking how the content really hit home and reflected what they felt every single day. Watching the numbers climb in real time was mind-blowing.

By week's end, the video had rocketed to one million views. I thought, *If they like this, then I have eleven years of material I can't wait to unload!*

I wasted no time producing the next video. I needed to strike while the iron was hot. After a few more videos with millions of views to follow, I realized that God had truly blessed me with an idea that would allow teachers to connect with what they really wish they could say. Just the thought of something so routine, speaking on behalf of a nation of educators, was the best feeling in the world. Finally, something that Teachers could call their own and use as a stress release.

A Teacher's Pet Peeve

The struggle is real.

To many people, this chapter will probably sound like a petulant rant about managing first world problems at work. So, before I begin, let me acknowledge that I am fully aware that workers in various occupations are faced with countless unwanted and frustrating issues each and every day. Some employees even face hazardous work conditions or risk their lives doing their jobs. None of that is not lost upon me, and I salute each and every person who must contend with precarious situations to earn a living. However, when it comes to handling circumstances that make one's job more difficult than it has to be, it's relative. What may be a carefree walk in the park for one staffer could be a combat crawl through a war zone for another. With that said, I need to get this off my chest.

As public school educators, we face tons of challenges we wish we didn't have to deal with. Some of the issues are more annoying than demanding. A few that come to mind (and you do not necessarily have to be a teacher to relate) include what can only be summed up as an internal affairs raid on our classrooms. During the school day, administrators sometimes execute walk-throughs. Basically, the bosses come in looking to catch a teacher engaging in activity they have no business working on. Yeah, I said it! Of course, the higher-ups insist there is nothing nefarious about the visits, and they are only intended to positively reinforce a teacher's role in the classroom and assess the kids while they are engaged in a structured task.

However, during this surveillance—I mean, as we are being "observed"—the administrator strides by oblivious to all the children who are on task and enthusiastic about the lesson and makes a beeline for the one student sitting in the back of the room, facing the wall. Yes, that one boy or girl who would rather color, mark up the desk, nod off, or stare off into space than follow directions. The child that has no clue what lesson is being taught. And it is not that we, as teachers, don't care. We do. We just resign ourselves to the fact that, if that student is not disruptive, it benefits everyone. He or she is pretty much having a good day. Still, the administrator, who is typically unaware that this dynamic exists or chooses to ignore it because they have an agenda, approaches the apathetic pupil and poses the burning question: "What are y'all working on in class today?"

News flash: he does not know! Sure, he may not be focused on the task at hand, but he is focused. He is not getting in the way of the other students' learning, and he is not interrupting me as I teach. He is coloring quietly. Hell, I hardly know he's even in the classroom. Administrators ignore the fact that the other 95 percent of the kids are doing what they are supposed to and give us bad evaluations when they should be praising us for making progress with the kid everyone gave up on. He's finally started coloring inside the lines. That's an A for him!

Let me put the above scenario in an even greater context. A student is placed in my sixth-grade class. He reads at a second-grade level. Through painstaking effort, I get him to a fourth-grade reading level by the end of the school year. Instead of praising me, the district threatens my job because the state says I failed to meet the standard. How am I, or any educator, supposed to be encouraged? How is this positive reinforcement?

You know what motivates us? More pay. Job security. Appreciation. Telling us our jobs are on the line does not spur enthusiasm.

Some other exasperating behavior that needs to change: adding a new student to the class at the end of the semester. Just leaving him at the door like an abandoned baby. No background information. No heads-up about possible learning disabilities. Nothing.

Administrators who schedule last-minute mandatory meetings about every little thing have to stop. Just stop. Most are an exercise in futility. A lot of the times, those meaningless, unproductive gatherings cover a subject that could've easily been emailed to everyone. The time would be better served in the classroom.

We *hate* being accountable for things that should not be under our purview. Setting goals for each student, turning in lesson plans weeks in advance, outside duty, bus duty, and cafeteria duty make me want to scream, "Damn a duty! Why can't we just work on being the best teachers we can be? These onerous obligations are distractions!" And when all is said and done, what do we get for it? Very little. It seems like our only reward is "jeans day." Really? Come on. We spend our days forming young minds and preparing children for the future, and all you can come up with to say, "Good job" is dishing out a denim pass? Let's be reasonable, shall we? The reward does not match the responsibilities.

While I am at it, it bears mentioning that we do not like being "volun-told" to do everything and anything outside of teaching. Yes, I just made up that word. Teachers get signed up as heads of committees without any notice. If we refuse, we risk being blacklisted and hassled for the remainder of the year. I am far too committed to my students to be committed to a committee. *Just let us be.* Let us be great. Let us bring our own ideas to the table. Let us be autonomous. Let us be teachers. Educators make it their life's work to become familiar with the learning abilities of their students—more so than any administrator. Stop stepping on our ideas and disregarding our vision because it does not qualify as your favorite cop-out: "Research shows." That's tantamount to going to get your car detailed, and it rains as soon as you pull out of the car wash. It feels like the biggest waste of time and energy. It depletes the spirit of educators when their passion is snuffed out.

If anybody is listening, I have one thing to say: Help! Help us be better teachers. Help us be better role models. Help us honor our profession by allowing us to do our jobs.

What Good Mentors Really Say When You Need Direction

WHEN THE "WHAT TEACHERS REALLY SAY" videos started gaining momentum, I began receiving emails and comments on my social media posts from educators who thanked me for giving teachers everywhere a voice. Most were grateful that I was able to sum up exactly what they were thinking in less than one minute. The fact that the clips were funny and satirical was an added bonus. It began to feel like a huge responsibility for one person.

I was a teacher and a comic who simply wanted to make entertaining videos that described my experiences as an educator and served as a release—a way to let off steam while I tried to make sense of my life. Obviously, I had tons of material. Teacher-training sessions in the summertime could have been an entire series of its own. I could have recorded hours of programming about returning to work after spring break. Let's not even discuss my disdain for (and consequently my treasure chest of ammunition about) professional development courses. I think those videos may be among the most popular.

The videos were—and hopefully continue to be—relatable, and from the feedback I received, spot-on. However, I never set out to be a "voice for teachers." It was hard enough to articulate my own personal anxiety as an educator. Trying to express the frustration of an entire industry would have triggered a complete meltdown. I would've gone completely crazy. Hell, I was already halfway there.

I remember sitting at home before I started making the videos and traveling around the country with the Teachers Only tour, wondering if I was the only one who felt a sense of dread every night when I thought about going back to my classroom. I knew *most* teachers were not happy with the state of affairs in the industry. As a matter of fact, I took solace in the fact that teachers in every city had their own grievances. However, I no longer wanted to commiserate with my academic counterparts. I wanted out. I wanted a better life—with a decent wage and a promise of professional advancement. Above all, I wanted a job where the work I put in would result in some sense of fulfilment.

I was part of a group of superheroes (anyone who does not believe teachers are superheroes has no idea what we go through) who sacrifice everything from time to money to make a difference in the lives of children everywhere. I have yet to meet the man or woman who says they became a teacher for the fat paycheck and lavish lifestyle that come with the profession.

One night, I made the mistake of researching where Houston ranks among top-paying cities for teachers. I started googling statistics and jotting down the data. The more I searched, the lower my heart sank. For the record, googling teacher salaries when you are feeling down is about as bad as logging on to WebMD to diagnose inexplicable symptoms. The information you gather make you feel like death is around the corner—a step away from the pearly gates. I was going to meet Jesus, my Lord and Savior, broke as hell.

The average annual salary was depressingly low. Compared to the state average, H-town hovered somewhere around number seven on recruitment company Indeed's list of cities where it pays the most to be a teacher in the United States. For a single father weighed down by bills, debts, and worries, that result offered very little comfort. After all I had been through, and was going through, I felt I deserved more.

Man, there were times I felt guilty for desiring and praying for something other than seeing a new generation succeed. It took a long time for me to come to terms with the understanding that wanting more out of life did not mean I wanted *less* for the kids I taught. As a matter of fact, if I was not happy with the man I was becoming, how could I be expected to instill a sense of confidence, discipline, and love for learning in impressionable children? There is a quote by William Arthur Ward that has always stuck with me: "The mediocre teacher tells. The good teacher explains. The superior teacher demonstrates. The great teacher inspires." I did not have the will to "inspire." That was not fair to me or anybody's child.

Working for Fonville Middle School in the Houston Independent School District was stressful. I would rather have a cement enema than go to class somedays. I was mentally and physically stuck. There were no other job prospects—at least nothing as rewarding as helping kids. One of the biggest challenges I encountered at Fonville and other schools I worked in was callous administrations. If attitude reflects leadership, the professionals at the helm of our schools needed to work on their personal development. Who was evaluating their strengths and weaknesses? Where were their workshops? And I don't mean those two-day, one-and-done sessions teachers have to sit through. Those folks need a weeklong intensive focused on how to treat faculty (and staff) like human beings instead of machines.

Supervisors were rarely benevolent. Many had six-figure salaries and clearly were not being compensated for their obliging dispositions. I will never begrudge anyone their "come up," but I have a serious problem when professionals charged with encouraging teachers' growth shirk their responsibilities. Maybe this was ingrained in the school system or endemic to the academic hierarchy, but teachers—more often than not—had to fend for themselves. Running the district and overseeing schools was about business and not the needs of the educator. After two years at that particular school, I began feeling like it was us against them—and we were losing the fight.

I was also about to meet a new contender.

The rumor mill had been grinding for weeks. A new administrator had been assigned to our campus to call the shots in the Science Department and be in charge of the sixth-grade team. Basically, this person would be unavoidable. Chances are, they would echo the agenda I had come to expect from the district. The more things change, the more they remain the same.

My stomach flipped when I was told to report to a meeting with our department's new administrator. I wanted to ask why I could not just read the minutes of the last meeting we had with the former head of the team. The new person would probably just regurgitate the company line or try to introduce "new programs" that were nothing but old programs with new acronyms.

Do I really need to be there to hear this?

Well, yeah. I had no choice. Who was I kidding by talking all that mess? My inner monologue was about to get me fired. Sure enough, I made my way to the meeting.

As I approached the conference room, I stopped outside the door, confused. *Am I hearing things? Is that laughter? Pleasant conversation? Hints of mirth? How is this possible? At a meeting?*

I entered the room, and there she was. Dr. Karen Jackson was sitting at the head of the class. She was confident, affable, and approachable, and she was socializing with the teachers in our group as if she was not in a position of power. Her smile and mannerisms were so genuine and inviting. She spoke with each person as if we were all old friends.

When Dr. Jackson and I talked, she admitted that she had heard a lot about me.

I thought, *Oh boy—my days are numbered.*

After reassuring me the observations about my performance were positive, she began to outline the agenda she was putting forth and affirmed that she was on our side. She intended to fight for teachers and not against them. Dr. Jackson told me that there were no insurmountable obstacles or issues that could not be resolved as long as all parties communicated and remained receptive.

I'm sure many of you can relate to what was going through my mind, especially if you are a teacher. We've heard it all before. These public servants come in promising the world, eager to form curriculums, goals, and budgets. They enact performance measures to ensure that educators meet personal and professional goals. I'm not sure what "ruler" they use to "measure" these standards, but in my experience, most need to be recalibrated.

My personal favorite was supervisors who came in and wanted to hold hands, sing "Kumbaya," and convince their unwitting minions that administrators and faculty would work together to carve a path to success for all. Up until the day I met Dr. Jackson, I never believed a single word. But after looking into her eyes and listening to her speak, I could tell she meant every single word. I felt something I had not experienced in a very long time: hope.

Dr. Jackson raised the bar, and she redefined it and provided us with the tools and opportunities to make it attainable. She was a teacher's dream: an authority figure who cared. She understood the demands I faced as a single father and never gave me a hard time when I needed to leave early to pick my son up from school (provided I did not make it a habit or allow it to interfere with my class schedule). I'd never had that before.

I felt comfortable confiding in Dr. Jackson about my personal issues. She was extremely attentive and nonjudgmental. The day I explained how my mother played an integral role in shaping my character and shared that losing her devastated me beyond words, she literally threw open her arms. I fell in, tears flowing. I did not realize how much I needed that embrace. The words she whispered as she hugged me tightly nearly leveled me: "I will be your mother." Time stopped. For a split second, it was like hearing my mom's voice again. I missed her so much. It was surreal. This person I barely knew had accessed my painful past and the memories I kept buried deep. I kept those secrets bottled up tightly, but with her, they gushed like water from a geyser!

As far as I was concerned, working with Dr. Jackson had the hand of God all over it. It was a much-needed reality check. I was becoming far too jaded and cynical. I believed no one in power could be trusted and that people in charge conspired to undermine the people they managed. It was a heavy burden to bear. In my line of work, those in positions of authority consistently did all they could to hold me back. God found a way to prove otherwise. By bringing Karen into our lives, he showed me that all people are not cut from the same cloth. In fact, some leaders are not intent on domineering over those in their charge and choose instead to be examples. She encouraged all of us to expect better and believe the best in people. I discovered that all administrators are not adversaries, all supervisors are not enemies, and the men and women who oversee our districts and our schools are not all judgmental, self-serving, or trying to put my career in a choke hold.

Dr. Jackson embodied what every person in a position of power should aspire to with her motivational management style. I'd never worked so hard for an administrator in my life. She created an environment that encouraged productivity. She made teaching worth it again. I actually looked forward to going to school, preparing lesson plans, and challenging my students to excel and invest in their futures.

I hope that everyone reading this chapter finds someone like Dr. Jackson on their journey. She changed my life and inspired me to reach higher. At the time, I had no idea I would be sharing this story with hundreds of thousands of people. Today, I can say with certainty that I probably would not have had the courage to stick it out were it not for Dr. Jackson. If I had given up, this tour and this book would not have been possible.

Educators Need Educators

You are never too old—or experienced—to learn something new.

I had been teaching for a decade and become acutely aware of an aloofness among teachers. Interaction between educators was often cold. When two or three gathered, there was a shady vibe among them. (Forgive the biblical reference, especially since very little about teacher networking reflected anything godly). I've never fully understood what caused the rifts. I suppose the pressure of the job combined with the autonomy of the position played a role.

Our day-to-day business didn't lend itself to camaraderie or cordial association. For the most part, it was every man and woman for himself or herself. Each person was responsible for their own lesson plan, assignments, and curriculum. Basically, your classroom was your obligation and your domain. There was little time to peek into another teacher's territory and offer a helping hand because our hands were always full. That train of thought was the underpinning of selfish, jealous, entitled, and sometimes even pompous behavior. Oh, and do *not* let some of those teachers realize any level of success in academia compared to their counterparts. They wear awards, promotions, and recognition from higher-ups like badges of honor. Decorated faculty consider themselves superior and rarely deign to lavish attention on struggling educators who are trying to survive a semester. That level of hubris does not belong in a classroom, and it does nothing to forge a bond among colleagues.

Things got so bad that I became borderline reclusive. I only considered my work and my goals. I morphed into who I hated, which was not conducive to achieving what I consider the ultimate goal of teaching: teamwork to help the kids work should be the cornerstone of our work. It is one of few professions where unity is essential. They say, "It takes a village to raise a child." Well, in our world, the school should be a "village." Unfortunately, for whatever reason, we don't support each other. Ultimately, the kids are the ones who suffer.

I've witnessed teachers with phenomenal ideas retreat—deflated by feelings of self-doubt, inadequacy, and isolation simply—because they believed their objectives would not be well received. They were concerned their actions, however well-intentioned, would not be accepted by their peers. Some hesitated to share input because they were convinced so-called veteran teachers would dismiss new (out-of-the-box) methods that didn't conform to the norm.

I speak from experience.

When the Principal reassigned me (under protest) to teach eighth-grade science, I floundered like a fish out of water. I knew nothing about the curriculum and set aside pride to ask for assistance. After all, the sixth-grade team I worked with prior to being transferred had always been supportive. We all looked out for each other. If one of us succeeded, it would bode well for the collective. In the end, we banded together for the sake of the students.

I expected my new team to subscribe to the same synergy. That would be a resounding *hell no*. Quite the contrary. I asked one of the teachers if she would mind sharing her lesson plan, and she informed me, in no uncertain terms, that I needed to create my own. And trust me, she did not say, "You will never get acclimated to the new program if you don't at least try to manage it yourself." It was more like she said, "Why the hell would I give you my lesson plan? I'm not here to hold your hand. You're a teacher. Act like one." It was pretty rude, definitely harsh, and completely uncalled for. Others shared her point of view.

By day's end, rumors were running rampant that Mr. Brown didn't have a clue. They framed my request for help as a sign of ineptitude, an indication I did not know how or what to teach. I leaned on a fellow educator for guidance, and she broadcast a narrative that set me up for failure. I struggled to find resources on my own. I walked up and down the eighth-grade hallways dodging whispers, giggles, and side glances from grown men and women who were acting more like school bullies than professionals charged with the care of our kids. Their brutal survival-of-the-fittest mentality was downright shameful and completely counterproductive.

Despite the lack of cooperation, my teaching career flourished. I got my bearings, gained an understanding of the curriculum, developed great lesson plans, and ended the year on a positive note. I found firmer ground. More importantly, I learned a valuable lesson: people (especially some teachers) can be cruel, but I do not have to follow their game plan. I made it a point to always be available to any teacher who needed my assistance. If a fellow educator needs advice, resources, or any attention whatsoever to help them better serve the students, I will be there.

I despise narrow-minded teachers who withhold knowledge or deny others access to the tools they need to function. Asking for help in a foreign environment—regardless of your level of experience—is humiliating enough. Why on earth would you further degrade someone who is in the trenches with you by belittling them? How can you sleep at night after crippling someone professionally? That person more than likely is in a position you were once in. Those actions are unacceptable. They fly in the face of decency and good stewardship. Treat others the way you want to be treated. You never know when you will find yourself on the other side, treading water and looking for a lifeline.

I have taken time off from teaching. The year I returned to the classroom after I "retired" the first time, I taught math. I struggled, but after intense preparation, 80 percent of my kids went on to pass the math portion of the state standardized test. I never taught the subject or produced passing scores before. I brimmed with pride—but never arrogance. I knew I owed it all to a group of teachers who stepped up to support me for the first time in my teaching career.

Unfortunately, there continues to be a major division among educators. As long as the condition persists, any meaningful change will elude us. A school's success is predicated on the fellowship of its teachers and not estrangement between educators. Point blank, period.

Exceptional leadership is a plus. A clear focus is a plus. Awesome resources are a plus. However, nothing will ever be more effective than an environment where teachers encourage each other.

In Honor of My Father

MY FATHER DIED IN 2018. Prior to writing this chapter, it was not easy to find the words—or the heart—to speak positively about him. The subject has always been difficult for me. For years, whenever the topic of my dad came up, it would dredge up painful memories and further contaminate open wounds. I asked myself if I should even include the topic in this book.

I am sharing my life story in an effort to inspire others to keep pursuing their dreams and to motivate fellow educators who have bought into the notion that they are trapped in a thankless job that takes more than it gives. After working as a teacher, I know that is not the case. The job can be a brain drain, and there are days when it can deplete your spirits. However, it is one of the most fulfilling jobs out there. I try to remain positive, and my character plays an integral role in how I approach each day. That brings me to the reason I chose to write about my relationship with my father in this book. Good or bad, he helped shape who I am. And even though the relationship was rocky, I am grateful for what it taught me about life and about myself.

While I was growing up, my father was absent. I was raised by my mother and my grandmother, which was not uncommon in my community. Most of the kids around me accepted that as part of our reality. To have a father in the home was the exception and not the rule. We did not know any better. Fortunately, I was surrounded by admirable father figures throughout my life. Knowing I had a father out there who would rather remain estranged really messed with my mind. It did something to my spirit too. I didn't realize it so much as a child, but the emptiness became more acute as I got older, especially when I saw other young men who had loving, stable patriarchal households. I don't care how tough you think you are—it hurts. Badly.

I learned of my father's passing during the Teachers Only tour. We were literally basking in the glow of one of the most exciting times of our professional lives. My team and I were surrounded by loyal fans, traveling to remarkable cities, making new friends, and creating incredible memories. God was not just showing out—he was showing off. When I received the news that my dad died, I thought, *Damn. Just as my life is starting to make sense and I am finally in control of my future—and in a good place mentally and spiritually—here comes the added chaos.* I know it sounds cruel, but given the level of dysfunction that typified our sporadic contact, my irreverence was warranted.

I altered my tour schedule to attend the funeral. I sincerely wanted to pay my respects. Given the circumstances, I was beset by anxiety and uncertainty. I barely knew him, and I was even less acquainted with his family. It was one of many times I wished I could have talked to my mom. I needed her insight and comforting words. I can't say with assurance that she would have kind things to say about him, but I am positive she would have at least allayed my reservations. *Oh well. Since Mom is gone, I am on my own here.*

When I arrived at the funeral, I encountered an unanticipated dilemma. I would not feel comfortable sitting next to my father's family. Except for his son and daughter, I didn't know them at all. I chose a seat way in the back where I could view the casket from a distance. I surveyed the church and did some low-key people watching (I didn't want to come off like a creep). I avoided making eye contact with anyone in particular as I tried to determine which mourners were related to my father. It was an odd feeling to be in a room full of relatives and still feel so alone.

From my seat, I spotted a wall overflowing with pictures of my father depicted in varying degrees of revelry: laughing, hugging, and engaging with a variety of different people, young and old. It was clearly a poignantly arranged collage of friends and family posing with a man who appeared to be beloved. I wondered if there were any pictures of me in that lovingly arranged array. Now, I could not take in all the shots from my solitary perch, but who was I fooling? I know there were none.

The name above the pictorial tribute caught my attention. My father's middle name was Royce! This seems like such a random observation and not necessarily a fact that should have garnered such a visceral reaction from me, yet it reminded me how little I knew about him.

During the service, I found out even more snippets. He could cook a mean brisket? I saw a lot of people nod and smile knowingly when the pastor brought that up. My father loved the song "What's the 411?" by Mary J. Blige? I definitely didn't see that coming. He was also a big fan of jazz music. Wynton Marsalis, Miles Davis, Thelonious Monk, and John Coltrane were some of his favorite artists from that genre. As those near and dear to him shared these personal reflections, I could feel my loss deepening. It was not because my father was dead; it was because I had nothing to share. I had no memories that would make his loved ones laugh or cry.

A feeling of profound regret began to settle in. I remember thinking we would have gotten along so well. *All that time wasted, and I will never get it back.* My sadness was suspended by a moment of levity when I learned that his nickname was "Catfish." For some reason, that made me smile. I shook my head wistfully and whispered "Catfish" to myself over and over.

My emotions were all over the place. I struggled with feelings of regret, anger, and pettiness. (God was not done with me yet). I almost walked out. Twice. My inner monologue was savage: *Why are you still here? That dude left you to fend for yourself out here! You made it without him, but here you are. You're sitting in the back of the church at his funeral because you know you don't fit in with the people he really loved! Where is your dignity?* Man, the conflict between my ego and my Christianity was raging out of control. What can I say? I'm a work in progress.

As the hours passed, I started to enjoy all the nostalgia. As people strolled down memory lane, I walked alongside them, carefully collecting pieces of their recollections and hoping to somehow create my own image of the man. I drew upon their experiences, and in my mind, I fashioned what I felt was a decent version of the father I wish I had known. I walked away from the funeral right before the viewing. I wanted my final memory to be when I last saw him, alive and well.

Bruce Lee said, "Humility forms the basis of honor just as the low ground forms the foundation of a high elevation." It's been some time since I sat in the back of that church and paid my respects to the man I once loathed. It's been said that time heals all wounds. Well, the temporal continuance is as much an intellectual salve as it is a mental and spiritual fix. I've painfully and slowly started to grasp the true meaning of honor. Lord knows it's not always an easy—or popular—decision to pay homage to someone. Most times, it is not predicated on their greatness or their life's work. It is usually a personal choice.

I don't know why my father chose not to be part of my life. Who knows? It might not have been his decision. My faith tells me that if it was meant for my dad to be present when I was growing up, God would have made a way for it to happen. Whatever the reason, I need to release my hurt and anger. I will simply respect and honor the fact that he was my dad. Nothing will change that. That rationale is cathartic in that it frees me of the negativity and resentment I've been storing in my heart for years. I find myself reflecting on my relationship with my own son. One thing is certain: I would never leave my boy. If I did go anywhere, he'd be right by my side. That is nonnegotiable.

I have been blessed with numerous role models, including men who taught in the schools I attended and coaches who guided me through my love of sports. In many public schools, kids are growing up with minimal or no parental support at home. Thankfully, I've been a father figure to several of my students, and I know the results have been positive. If I harbored ill will toward my father, I would've lost sight of how important it is to play an active, positive role in the lives of the students under my watch for eight hours a day.

To my dad: Rest in heaven. Understand that I understand. I love you just as if I saw you every day as child.

A Message to My Fellow Teachers

FIRST OF ALL, I WANT to welcome you to the teaching profession. I am honored to be in such outstanding company.

Throughout your career, you will question your decision to become an educator. There will be days you ask, "Is this is for me," and others when you declare, "I definitely made the right decision." Your attitude will typically reflect the kind of day, week, month, or semester you are having. It sounds unpredictable and may cause you to doubt your judgment—and maybe regret all the money you spent to earn that degree and the student loans that will haunt you for years.

When skepticism creeps in, I urge you to focus on the positive. In order to do that, think back to when you were in school. Remember all the people who influenced you as a child? Remember the effect educators had on your life? Remember how they carried themselves? Use those memories as a guide. Incorporate the good you are able to glean from your recollections into your coursework and lesson plans. If it inspired you, chances are your students will benefit as well. Should you find yourself discouraged by negative memories, use that too. You now know what not to do. You have the advantage of knowing what doesn't resonate with kids and what turns them off. Consider yourself in tune with methods that reach children in meaningful ways. As a teacher, that is an enviable position to be in.

Please do not hesitate to integrate fresh ideas in your classroom. Just don't introduce them to colleagues too hastily. Some concepts will not be readily accepted. Everyone is not always open to innovative thinking. Many educators are creatures of habit. Change makes them uncomfortable. This is not intended to criticize those who prefer what they believe are tried-and-true methods of education. However, if you are aware you may face some pushback, you may be more inclined to shore up your proposals with hard and fast, factual, well-researched studies on why contemporary ideologies can also be successful. Sometimes the old guard just needs a little modern-day persuasion.

You will be told you have an opportunity to change the world one kid at a time. That is the best incentive. Getting there is not always easy. It all starts in the classroom. You will be asked to implement effective, strict, and favorable work habits. Simple enough, right? Not really. Here is what you may not hear. Those in the know—and the ones who are in charge—may not adequately convey the importance of classroom management or warn you that you will be expected to teach effectively while tangling with discipline issues. Not all students are cooperative. If any of this is addressed, specifics will not be expounded upon or detailed through modeling. Controlling your class is the key to teaching in a public school. The practice serves as the groundwork and foundation. Work at mastering techniques that will keep your kids engaged while driving your rules and expectations home until they become ingrained in their DNA. Once you have a disciplined learning environment, you can teach your kids anything. There is no other way around it. Classroom management is the key to a successful career.

Guard your passion. The district and different administrators will try to instill their rules, regulations, and nonnegotiable expectations. By all means, follow the guidelines, but do not let routines and deadlines dampen your dedication. Teaching with fervor will get you through those days when your career is mired in uncertainty.

Be wary of those who offer unsolicited advice. As a matter of fact, vet all counsel. Everyone does not have your best interests at heart. Some are decent, kindhearted human beings. Others are selfish and want only to outperform you.

You will hear both horror and success stories. Remain amenable to the positive. After a while, you will be able to distinguish between adversaries and those who are rooting for you. They are the ones who check on you, ask if you need anything, offer assistance, and share information that veterans are privy too in order to ease your challenges. Your mentor will likely be a member of your team—but don't rule out keeping to yourself occasionally. There is nothing wrong with being a loner. You will discover there is power in mystery.

Listen attentively and be slow to speak in meetings. That is an ideal time to learn.

There will be plenty of time to participate in the discourse when you are ready.

Finally, pay attention to how successful teachers carry themselves and run their classrooms, especially with regard to disciplinary measures.

As with any profession, you will encounter ups and downs. Treasure the highs—and do not be deterred by the lows. There will be countless blessings, so expect returns on your investment of time, commitment, and inspiration. The best reward? The students who will call you for years to come, thanking you for the role you played in their lives.

Once again, congratulations!

CPSIA information can be obtained
at www.ICGtesting.com
Printed in the USA
LVHW061232030319
609267LV00010B/34/P

9 781532 067914